MEETING NOTES

&

PLANNER

MY PLANS \ MEETING NOTES \ MEMORIES OF THE YEAR

ΔΣΘ

This is a work of fiction. Names, characters, places, and incidents either are the product of the author's imagination or are used fictitiously. Any resemblance to actual persons, living or dead, events, or locales is entirely coincidental.

Book design by Dr. Sherrá M. Watkins
Sister WELLS Counseling, Coaching & Consulting, PLLC

ISBN 979-8-9855349-7-9

www.sisterwells.org

TABLE OF

Content

____

LET'S MAKE BEAUTIFUL MEMORIES AND HOPE THAT THIS YEAR WILL BE BLESSED WITH MANY SUCH OPPORTUNITIES.

Delta Sigma Theta Sorority, Inc.

THIS JOURNAL
Belongs To:

Name

___

Phone

___

Email

___

CHAPTER CONTACT LIST

Name
Phone
Email
Website
Address
Notes

Name
Phone
Email
Website
Address
Notes

Name
Phone
Email
Website
Address
Notes

Name
Phone
Email
Website
Address
Notes

Name
Phone
Email
Website
Address
Notes

Name
Phone
Email
Website
Address
Notes

Name
Phone
Email
Website
Address
Notes

Name
Phone
Email
Website
Address
Notes

Name
Phone
Email
Website
Address
Notes

Name
Phone
Email
Website
Address
Notes

IMPORTANT THINGS TO REMEMBER

Chapter Name:	
Initiation Date:	
Founders' Day:	

THINGS I WOULD LIKE TO ACCOMPLISH THIS YEAR

YEARLY EVENTS

JANUARY	FEBRUARY	MARCH

APRIL	MAY	JUNE

JULY	AUGUST	SEPTEMBER

OCTOBER	NOVEMBER	DECEMBER

CALENDAR

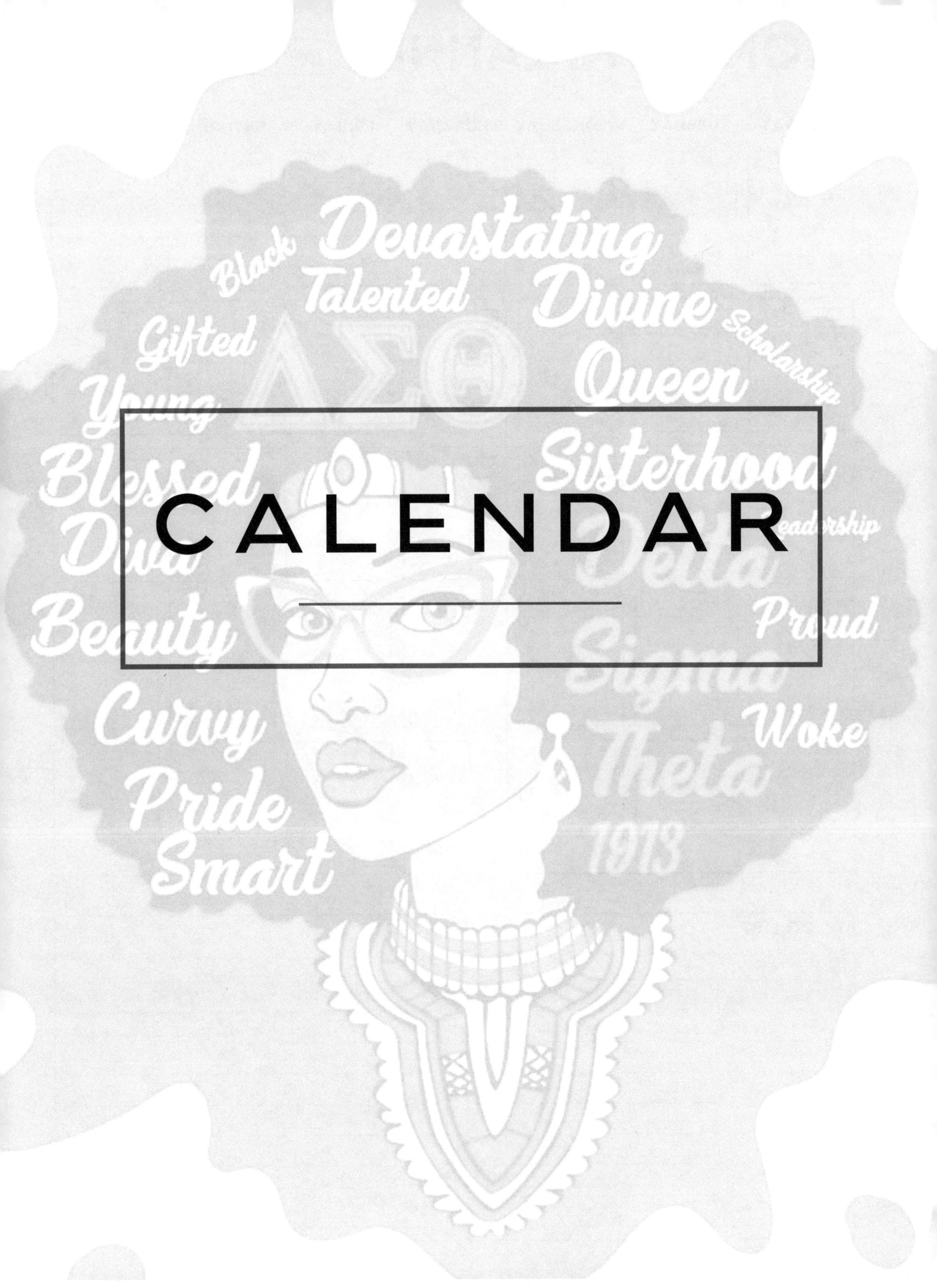
Black
Devastating
Talented
Divine
Scholarship
Gifted
ΔΣΘ
Queen
Young
Blessed
Sisterhood
Diva
Leadership
Delta
Beauty
Proud
Sigma
Curvy
Woke
Theta
Pride
1913
Smart

MONTHLY PLANNER

MONTH:

MONDAY	TUESDAY	WEDNESDAY	THURSDAY	FRIDAY	SATURDAY	SUNDAY

TO DO LIST:

NOTES:

MEETING NOTES

DATE -

AGENDA -

MEETING NOTES -

ACTION PLAN -

TASK(S)	TASK(S) OWNER	TIMELINE

Monthly Review

MONTH

TOP ACCOMPLISHMENTS

HIGHLIGHTS

SETBACKS

THINGS TO LEARN

THINGS TO CHANGE

START

STOP

CONTINUE

NEXT MONTH PRIORITIES

NOTES

Date : / /

MONTHLY PLANNER

MONTH:

MONDAY	TUESDAY	WEDNESDAY	THURSDAY	FRIDAY	SATURDAY	SUNDAY

TO DO LIST:

NOTES:

MEETING NOTES

DATE -

AGENDA -

MEETING NOTES -

ACTION PLAN -

TASK(S)	TASK(S) OWNER	TIMELINE

Monthly Review

MONTH

TOP ACCOMPLISHMENTS

HIGHLIGHTS

SETBACKS

THINGS TO LEARN

THINGS TO CHANGE

START

STOP

CONTINUE

NEXT MONTH PRIORITIES

NOTES

Date : / /

MONTHLY PLANNER

MONTH:

MONDAY	TUESDAY	WEDNESDAY	THURSDAY	FRIDAY	SATURDAY	SUNDAY

TO DO LIST:

NOTES:

MEETING NOTES

DATE -

AGENDA -

MEETING NOTES -

ACTION PLAN -

TASK(S)	TASK(S) OWNER	TIMELINE

Monthly Review

MONTH

TOP ACCOMPLISHMENTS

HIGHLIGHTS

SETBACKS

THINGS TO LEARN

THINGS TO CHANGE

START

STOP

CONTINUE

NEXT MONTH PRIORITIES

NOTES

Date : / /

MONTHLY PLANNER

MONTH:

MONDAY	TUESDAY	WEDNESDAY	THURSDAY	FRIDAY	SATURDAY	SUNDAY

TO DO LIST:

NOTES:

MEETING NOTES

DATE -

AGENDA -

MEETING NOTES -

ACTION PLAN -

TASK(S)	TASK(S) OWNER	TIMELINE

Monthly Review

MONTH

TOP ACCOMPLISHMENTS

HIGHLIGHTS

SETBACKS

THINGS TO LEARN

THINGS TO CHANGE

START

STOP

CONTINUE

NEXT MONTH PRIORITIES

NOTES

Date : / /

MONTHLY PLANNER

MONTH:

MONDAY	TUESDAY	WEDNESDAY	THURSDAY	FRIDAY	SATURDAY	SUNDAY

TO DO LIST:

NOTES:

MEETING NOTES

DATE -

AGENDA -

MEETING NOTES -

ACTION PLAN -

TASK(S)	TASK(S) OWNER	TIMELINE

Monthly Review

MONTH

TOP ACCOMPLISHMENTS

HIGHLIGHTS

SETBACKS

THINGS TO LEARN

THINGS TO CHANGE

START

STOP

CONTINUE

NEXT MONTH PRIORITIES

NOTES

Date : / /

MONTHLY PLANNER

MONTH:

MONDAY	TUESDAY	WEDNESDAY	THURSDAY	FRIDAY	SATURDAY	SUNDAY

TO DO LIST:

NOTES:

MEETING NOTES

DATE -

AGENDA -

MEETING NOTES -

ACTION PLAN -

TASK(S)	TASK(S) OWNER	TIMELINE

Monthly Review

MONTH

TOP ACCOMPLISHMENTS

HIGHLIGHTS

SETBACKS

THINGS TO LEARN

THINGS TO CHANGE

START

STOP

CONTINUE

NEXT MONTH PRIORITIES

NOTES

Date : / /

MONTHLY PLANNER

MONTH:

MONDAY	TUESDAY	WEDNESDAY	THURSDAY	FRIDAY	SATURDAY	SUNDAY

TO DO LIST:

NOTES:

MEETING NOTES

DATE -

AGENDA -

MEETING NOTES -

ACTION PLAN -

TASK(S)	TASK(S) OWNER	TIMELINE

Monthly Review

MONTH

TOP ACCOMPLISHMENTS

HIGHLIGHTS

SETBACKS

THINGS TO LEARN

THINGS TO CHANGE

START

STOP

CONTINUE

NEXT MONTH PRIORITIES

NOTES

Date : / /

MONTHLY PLANNER

MONTH:

MONDAY	TUESDAY	WEDNESDAY	THURSDAY	FRIDAY	SATURDAY	SUNDAY

TO DO LIST:

NOTES:

MEETING NOTES

DATE -

AGENDA -

MEETING NOTES -

ACTION PLAN -

TASK(S)	TASK(S) OWNER	TIMELINE

Monthly Review

MONTH

TOP ACCOMPLISHMENTS

HIGHLIGHTS

SETBACKS

THINGS TO LEARN

THINGS TO CHANGE

START

STOP

CONTINUE

NEXT MONTH PRIORITIES

NOTES

Date :   /   /

MONTHLY PLANNER

MONTH:

MONDAY	TUESDAY	WEDNESDAY	THURSDAY	FRIDAY	SATURDAY	SUNDAY

TO DO LIST:

- [ ]
- [ ]
- [ ]
- [ ]
- [ ]
- [ ]
- [ ]
- [ ]
- [ ]

NOTES:

MEETING NOTES

DATE -

AGENDA -

MEETING NOTES -

ACTION PLAN -

TASK(S)	TASK(S) OWNER	TIMELINE

Monthly Review

MONTH

TOP ACCOMPLISHMENTS

HIGHLIGHTS

SETBACKS

THINGS TO LEARN

THINGS TO CHANGE

START

STOP

CONTINUE

NEXT MONTH PRIORITIES

NOTES

Date :   /   /

MONTHLY PLANNER

MONTH:

MONDAY	TUESDAY	WEDNESDAY	THURSDAY	FRIDAY	SATURDAY	SUNDAY

TO DO LIST:

NOTES:

MEETING NOTES

DATE -

AGENDA -

MEETING NOTES -

ACTION PLAN -

TASK(S)	TASK(S) OWNER	TIMELINE

Monthly Review

MONTH

TOP ACCOMPLISHMENTS

HIGHLIGHTS

SETBACKS

THINGS TO LEARN

THINGS TO CHANGE

START

STOP

CONTINUE

NEXT MONTH PRIORITIES

NOTES

Date : / /

MONTHLY PLANNER

MONTH:

MONDAY	TUESDAY	WEDNESDAY	THURSDAY	FRIDAY	SATURDAY	SUNDAY

TO DO LIST:

NOTES:

MEETING NOTES

DATE -

AGENDA -

MEETING NOTES -

ACTION PLAN -

TASK(S)	TASK(S) OWNER	TIMELINE

Monthly Review

MONTH

TOP ACCOMPLISHMENTS

HIGHLIGHTS

SETBACKS

THINGS TO LEARN

THINGS TO CHANGE

START

STOP

CONTINUE

NEXT MONTH PRIORITIES

NOTES

Date : / /

MONTHLY PLANNER

MONTH:

MONDAY	TUESDAY	WEDNESDAY	THURSDAY	FRIDAY	SATURDAY	SUNDAY

TO DO LIST:

NOTES:

MEETING NOTES

DATE -

AGENDA -

MEETING NOTES -

ACTION PLAN -

TASK(S)	TASK(S) OWNER	TIMELINE

Monthly Review

MONTH

TOP ACCOMPLISHMENTS

HIGHLIGHTS

SETBACKS

THINGS TO LEARN

THINGS TO CHANGE

START

STOP

CONTINUE

NEXT MONTH PRIORITIES

NOTES

Date :   /   /

1-Year Review

MONTH

TOP ACCOMPLISHMENTS

HIGHLIGHTS

SETBACKS

THINGS TO LEARN

THINGS TO CHANGE

START

STOP

CONTINUE

NEXT YEAR PRIORITIES

MONTHLY PLANNER

MONTH:

MONDAY	TUESDAY	WEDNESDAY	THURSDAY	FRIDAY	SATURDAY	SUNDAY

TO DO LIST:

NOTES:

THINGS I WOULD LIKE TO ACCOMPLISH THIS YEAR

YEARLY EVENTS

JANUARY	FEBRUARY	MARCH

APRIL	MAY	JUNE

JULY	AUGUST	SEPTEMBER

OCTOBER	NOVEMBER	DECEMBER

NOTES

Date :   /   /

Program & Events IDEAS

Resources Needed

Resources Needed

Program & Events IDEAS

Resources Needed

Resources Needed

Fundraising IDEAS

Resources Needed

Resources Needed

Fundraising IDEAS

Resources Needed

Resources Needed

Service IDEAS

(Community Service)

Resources Needed

Resources Needed

Service IDEAS

(Community Service)

Resources Needed

Resources Needed

PLANNING AN EVENT

Project Planner

Deadline: _______________

PROJECT INFO ____

____

GOAL(S):

MEETING SCHEDULE:

TEAM MEMBERS:

MILESTONES:

TASKS	ASSIGNED TO	DEADLINE

Project Budget

BUDGET PLANNER

Date: ______________________

S S M T W T F

Main Income:

Other Source:

Total:

Estimate:

Expenses:

Overview	Budget	Expenses	Difference
Total Income			
Total Estimate			
Total Expense			

PROJECT EXPENSES	✔	PROJECT EXPENSES	✔
	○		○
	○		○
	○		○
	○		○
	○		○
	○		○
	○		○
	○		○
	○		○

Project Notes

REVIEW PLANNER

Date: ----------------------

S S M T W T F

Meeting Topic

Presenter

Objective

Discussion Notes | Agenda

Project Review

MY JOURNAL

Date: ______________________

S S M T W T F

Project Planner

Deadline: ____________________

PROJECT INFO ____

____

GOAL(S):

MEETING SCHEDULE:

TEAM MEMBERS:

MILESTONES:

TASKS	ASSIGNED TO	DEADLINE

Project Budget

BUDGET PLANNER

Date: ______________________

S S M T W T F

Main Income:

Other Source:

Total:

Estimate:

Expenses:

Overview	Budget	Expenses	Difference
Total Income			
Total Estimate			
Total Expense			

PROJECT EXPENSES	✓	PROJECT EXPENSES	✓
	○		○
	○		○
	○		○
	○		○
	○		○
	○		○
	○		○
	○		○
	○		○

Project Notes

REVIEW PLANNER

Date: ______________________

S S M T W T F

Meeting Topic

Presenter

Objective

Discussion Notes | Agenda

Project Review

MY JOURNAL

Date: ____________

S S M T W T F

Project Planner

Deadline: ____________

PROJECT INFO ____________

____

GOAL(S):

MEETING SCHEDULE:

TEAM MEMBERS:

MILESTONES:

TASKS	ASSIGNED TO	DEADLINE

Project Budget

BUDGET PLANNER

Date: ____________________

S S M T W T F

Main Income:

Other Source:

Total:

Estimate:

Expenses:

Overview	Budget	Expenses	Difference
Total Income			
Total Estimate			
Total Expense			

PROJECT EXPENSES	✓	PROJECT EXPENSES	✓
	○		○
	○		○
	○		○
	○		○
	○		○
	○		○
	○		○
	○		○
	○		○

Project Notes

REVIEW PLANNER

Date: -----------------------

S S M T W T F

Meeting Topic

Presenter

Objective

Discussion Notes | Agenda

Project Review

MY JOURNAL

Date: ______________________

S S M T W T F

ADDITIONAL HELPFUL DOCUMENTS

THE MEMBER'S BILL OF RIGHTS

Each member has the right-

- To receive notices of all meetings. These notices should include any prior notices (bylaw amendments, etc.,) required to be given under the rules.
- To attend meetings, conferences, and conventions, and to expect them to start on time, a quorum being present, as well as to be properly conducted.
- To inspect the official records of the organization, but not at the inconvenience of the custodian of said records.
- To demand a copy of the by-laws, and to under-stand their covenants.
- To nominate and be nominated for office. To elect and be elected to office.
- To make inquiries, parliamentary or informational, and also any necessary requests.
- To enjoy reasonable quiet and peaceful attendance at meetings, which should be free from abuse, danger or menace to his safety, health, and integrity.
- To insist on the enforcement of the rules of the organization, as well as parliamentary law.
- To have a fair hearing before suspension, expulsion, or other penalties are applied.
- To receive, or inspect, an up-to-date copy of the by-laws, charter, rules and minutes of the organization.

OBLIGATIONS OF MEMBERS

Each member has the obligation-

- To understand that the written rules of the organization are superior to parliamentary law, and all members are governed by both.
- To pay his dues promptly.
- To accept majority rule on decisions.
- To accept officers elected, whether they are the member's personal choice or not, and to be loyal to those officers.
- To bring in new members and generally promote the objects and aims of the organization.
- To remember that when they fail to vote, they waive their rights and allow those who do vote to express the will of the majority.

What Kind of Member Are You?

Are you an active member, one who would be missed?

Or are you just contented, that your name is on the list?

Do you attend the meetings, and mingle with the flock?

Or do you meet in private, and criticize and mock?

Do you take an active part, to help the work along?

Or are you satisfied to be the kind that just belongs?

Do you work on committees and volunteer? As to this, there is no trick.

Or leave the work to just a few, and talk about the clique?

Come to the meetings often, and help with hand and heart.

Don't be just a member - But take an active part!

Think this over, member; you know what's right from wrong.

Are you an active member, or do you just belong?

~ Author Unknown

PARLIAMENTARY PROCEDURE

- Members must arrive on time for meetings and must not leave before adjournment unless for a very special reason and permission is obtained.
- Members must address the Chair before they begin speaking.
- Members should be prompt in seconding motions so as to bring business to the point of discussion.
- Members must address the member presiding, even temporarily, as Madame/Mister President. An acceptable alternative is Mister/ Madame Presiding Officer.
- Members should develop the art of listening. They should be well mannered, and attentive at all times.
- Members should instantly come to attention whenever the president raps the gavel.
- Members should not stand or otherwise wait for recognition when another member already has the floor.
- Members must sit at once if another member rises to a point of order.
- Members must never interrupt another member who is speaking, unless the rules give them that right.
- Members should not try to compete with the member who is speaking, by chit-chatting with their neighbors.
- Members should avoid personalities in speaking and strive to be brief, courteous, as well as correct.
- Members should not shout "Question." Their silence should indicate that they are ready to vote.
- Members should pay attention to the speaker and the business being conducted.
- Members should not make remarks outside the meeting which might interfere with the work being done by an officer or committee.
- Members should not sleep, doodle, or whisper while meetings are in progress.
- Members should not sit on their hands when applause is in order.
- Members should make contributions of their talents to the organization, and be willing to serve on committees.
- Members should be prompt in paying their dues.
- Members should cooperate with the elected officers of the organization.
- Members should discuss organization business during the meeting, but refrain from re-discussing it afterwards.
- Members should be loyal to the organization at all times, and be willing to offer friendly assistance to members.

REMEMBER:

- Each meeting is a play. Act out your part with correctness, so that you will someday be considered for a starring role.

ROBERTS RULES OF ORDER – SIMPLIFIED

Guiding Principles:

- Only one thing (motion) can be discussed at a time.
- Everyone has the right to participate in discussion if they wish.
- Everyone has the right to know what is going on at all times.
- Everyone should have a chance to speak before anyone may speak a second time.

A Motion:

- A motion is the topic under discussion (e.g., "I move that we discuss changing the meeting time").
- Before you can introduce a motion when no other motion is on the table, the president must recognize you first.
- Any member can introduce a motion when no other motion is on the table.
- A motion requires a second to be considered. If there is no second, the matter is not considered.
- Each motion must be disposed of (passed, defeated, tabled, referred to committee, or postponed indefinitely).

How To Implement Within The Meeting:

- You want to bring up a new idea before the group.
- After recognition by the president of the board, present your motion. A second is required for the motion to go to the floor for discussion, or consideration.

You want to change some of the wording in a motion under discussion.
After recognition by the president of the board, move to amend by

- adding words,
- striking words or
- striking and inserting words.

You like the idea of a motion being discussed, but you need to reword it beyond simple word changes.
Move to substitute your motion for the original motion. If it is seconded, discussion will continue on both motions and eventually the body will vote on which motion they prefer.

You want more study and/or investigation given to the idea being discussed.
Move to refer to a committee. Try to be specific as to the charge to the committee.

You want more time personally to study the proposal being discussed.
Move to postpone to a definite time or date.

You are tired of the current discussion.
Move to limit debate to a set period of time or to a set number of speakers. Requires a 2/3rds vote.

You have heard enough discussion.
Move to close the debate. Also referred to as calling the question. This cuts off discussion and brings the assembly to a vote on the pending question only. Requires a 2/3rds vote.

You believe the discussion has drifted away from the agenda and want to bring it back.
"Call for orders of the day."

You want to take a short break.
Move to recess for a set period of time.

ROBERTS RULES OF ORDER – SIMPLIFIED

You want to end the meeting.
Move to adjourn.

You are unsure the president announced the results of a vote correctly.
Without being recognized, call for a "division of the house." A roll call vote will then be taken.

You are confused about a procedure being used and want clarification.
Without recognition, call for "Point of Information" or "Point of Parliamentary Inquiry." The president of the board will ask you to state your question and will attempt to clarify the situation.

You have changed your mind about something that was voted on earlier in the meeting for which you were on the winning side.
Move to reconsider. If the majority agrees, the motion comes back on the floor as though the vote had not occurred.

You want to change an action voted on at an earlier meeting.
Move to rescind. If previous written notice is given, a simple majority is required. If no notice is given, a 2/3rds vote is required.

Unanimous Consent:
If a matter is considered relatively minor or opposition is not expected, a call for unanimous consent may be requested. If others make the request, the president of the board will repeat the request and then pause for objections.If none are heard, the motion passes.

- You may INTERRUPT a speaker for these reasons only:
    - to get information about business –point of information to get information about rules–parliamentary inquiry
    - if you can't hear, safety reasons, comfort, etc. –question of privilege
    - if you see a breach of the rules –point of order
    - if you disagree with the president's ruling – appeal
    - if you disagree with a call for Unanimous Consent – object

Quick Reference					
	Must Be Seconded	Open for Discussion	Can Be Amended	Vote Count Required to Pass	May Be Reconsidered or Rescinded
Main Motion	√	√	√	Majority	√
Amend Motion	√	√		Majority	√
Kill a Motion	√			Majority	√
Limit Debate	√		√	2/3rds	√
Close Discussion	√			2/3rds	√
Recess	√		√	Majority	
Adjourn (End Meeting)	√			Majority	
Refer to Committee	√	√	√	Majority	√
Postpone to a Later Time	√	√	√	Majority	√
Table	√			Majority	
Postpone Indefinitely	√	√	√	Majority	√

Reference: Cornell University. (n.d.). Roberts Rules of Order – Simplified. Retrieved from Ku-ni-eh. (n.d.). Roberts Rules of Order – The Rules. Retrieved from from https://ku-ni-eh.org/roberts-rules-of-order/

ROBERT'S RULES OF ORDER MOTIONS CHART

Based On: *Robert's Rules of Order Newly Revised* (10th Edition)

Part 1: Main Motions. These motions are listed in order of precedence. A motion can be introduced if it is higher on the chart than the pending motion.

PURPOSE:	YOU SAY:	CAN INTERRUPT?	REQUIRES A 2ND?	DEBATE?	CAN BE AMENDED?	VOTE REQUIRED?
Close the meeting	I move to adjourn	No	Yes	No	No	Majority
Take break	I move to recess for ...	No	Yes	No	Yes	Majority
Register complaint	I rise to a question of privilege	Yes	No	No	No	None
Make follow agenda	I call for the orders of the day	Yes	Np	No	No	None
Lay aside temporarily	I move to lay the question on the table	No	Yes	No	No	Majority
Close debate	I move the previous question	No	Yes	No	No	2/3
Limit or extend debate	I move that debate be limited to ...	No	Yes	No	Yes	2/3
Postpone to a certain time	I move to postpone the motion to ...	No	Yes	Yes	Yes	Majority
Refer to committee	I move to refer the motion to ...	No	Yes	Yes	Yes	Majority
Modify wording of motion	I move to amend the motion by ...	No	Yes	Yes	Yes	Majority
Kill main motion	I move that the motion be postponed indefinitely	No	Yes	Yes	No	Majority
Bring business before assembly (a main motion)	I move that [or "to"]	No	Yes	Yes	Yes	Majority

Part 2: Incidental Motions. No order of precedence. These motions arise incidentally and are decided immediately.

PURPOSE:	YOU SAY:	CAN INTERRUPT?	REQUIRES A 2ND?	DEBATE?	CAN BE AMENDED?	VOTE REQUIRED?
Enforce rules	Point of Order	Yes	No	No	No	None
Submit matter to assembly	I appeal from the decision of the chair	Yes	Yes	Varies	No	Majority
Suspend rules	I move to suspend the rules	No	Yes	No	No	2/3
Avoid main motion altogether	I object to the consideration of the question	Yes	No	No	No	2/3
Divide motion	I love to divide the question	No	Yes	No	Yes	Majority
Demand a rising vote	I move for a rising vote	Yes	No	No	No	None
Parliamentary law question	Parliamentary inquiry	Yes	No	No	No	None
Request for information	Point of information	Yes	No	No	No	None

Part 3: Motions That Bring a Question Again Before the Assembly. No order of precedence. Introduce only when nothing else is pending.

PURPOSE:	YOU SAY:	CAN INTERRUPT?	REQUIRES A 2ND?	DEBATE?	CAN BE AMENDED?	VOTE REQUIRED?
Take matter from table	I move to take from the table ...	No	Yes	No	No	Majority
Cancel previous action	I move to rescind ...	No	Yes	Yes	Yes	2/3 or Majority
Reconsider motion	I move to reconsider ...	No	Yes	Varies	No	Majority

THE RULES

- **Point of Privilege:** Pertains to noise, personal comfort, etc. – may interrupt only if necessary!
- **Parliamentary Inquiry:** Inquire as to the correct motion – to accomplish a desired result, or raise a point of order.
- **Point of Information:** Generally applies to information desired from the speaker: "I should like to ask the (speaker) a question."
- **Orders of the Day (Agenda):** A call to adhere to the agenda (a deviation from the agenda requires Suspending the Rules)
- **Point of Order:** Infraction of the rules, or improper decorum in speaking. Must be raised immediately after the error is made.
- **Main Motion:** Brings new business (the next item on the agenda) before the assembly.
- **Divide the Question:** Divides a motion into two or more separate motions (must be able to stand on their own).
- **Consider by Paragraph:** Adoption of paper is held until all paragraphs are debated and amended and entire paper is satisfactory; after all paragraphs are considered, the entire paper is then open to amendment, and paragraphs may be further amended. Any Preamble can not be considered until debate on the body of the paper has ceased.
- **Amend:** Inserting or striking out words or paragraphs, or substituting whole paragraphs or resolutions.
- **Withdraw/Modify Motion:** Applies only after question is stated; mover can accept an amendment without obtaining the floor.
- **Commit /Refer/Recommit to Committee:** State the committee to receive the question or resolution; if no committee exists include size of committee desired and method of selecting the members (election or appointment).
- **Extend Debate:** Applies only to the immediately pending question; extends until a certain time or for a certain period of time.
- **Limit Debate:** Closing debate at a certain time, or limiting to a certain period of time.
- **Postpone to a Certain Time:** State the time the motion or agenda item will be resumed.
- **Object to Consideration:** Objection must be stated before discussion or another motion is stated.
- **Lay on the Table:** Temporarily suspends further consideration/action on pending question; may be made after motion to close debate has carried or is pending.
- **Take from the Table:** Resumes consideration of item previously "laid on the table" – state the motion to take from the table.
- **Reconsider:** Can be made only by one on the prevailing side who has changed position or view.
- **Postpone Indefinitely:** Kills the question/resolution for this session – exception: the motion to reconsider can be made this session.
- **Previous Question:** Closes debate if successful – may be moved to "Close Debate" if preferred.
- **Informal Consideration:** Move that the assembly go into "Committee of the Whole" – informal debate as if in committee; this committee may limit number or length of speeches or close debate by other means by a 2/3 vote. All votes, however, are formal.
- **Appeal Decision of the Chair:** Appeal for the assembly to decide – must be made before other business is resumed; NOT debatable if relates to decorum, violation of rules or order of business.
- **Suspend the Rules:** Allows a violation of the assembly's own rules (except Constitution); the object of the suspension must be specified.

Reference: Ku-ni-eh. (n.d.). Roberts Rules of Order – The Rules. Retrieved from from https://ku-ni-eh.org/roberts-rules-of-order/

NOTES

Date : / /

NOTES

Date : / /

NOTES

Date : / /

NOTES

Date :   /   /

NOTES

Date :   /   /

NOTES

Date :   /   /

NOTES

Date : / /

NOTES

Date :   /   /

NOTES

Date :   /   /

NOTES

Date :   /   /

NOTES

Date : / /

NOTES

Date : / /

NOTES

Date :   /   /

MEETING NOTES
&
PLANNER

MY PLANS \ MEETING NOTES \ MEMORIES OF THE YEAR

Made in United States
Cleveland, OH
08 May 2025